Also by James Michael Matthew:

Prophecy before Vision

- ➤ Author Shout 2023 Reader Ready Award
- ➤ American Writing Award 2022
- ➤ New England Book Festival Award 2022
- ➤ New York Book Festival honorable mention 2022
- ➤ Full page feature in *Bookmad's* second quarter issue of 2023 and social media

Reject Self-Serving Power

- ➤ London Book Festival Award 2023
- ➤ The BREW Book Excellence Award 2023
- ➤ Indies Today Award 2022

Building the Climate Change Bridge

- ➤ LA Times Festival of Books 2023

Defeating the New Axis Powers

The Two $20 Trillion Opportunities

THE LEADERSHIP BROADCASTING COMPANY

THE DECISION-MAKING NETWORK

JAMES MICHAEL MATTHEW

ARCHWAY
PUBLISHING

Archway Publishing books may be ordered through booksellers or by contacting:

Archway Publishing
1663 Liberty Drive
Bloomington, IN 47403
www.archwaypublishing.com
844-669-3957

ISBN: 978-1-6657-4372-3 (sc)
ISBN: 978-1-6657-4370-9 (hc)
ISBN: 978-1-6657-4371-6 (e)

Library of Congress Control Number: 2023908532

Print information available on the last page.

Archway Publishing rev. date: 05/19/2023

This book is dedicated to all the people of the world who continue to lose confidence in the ability of their supposed leaders to provide anything resembling responsible leadership. From the abysmal approval ratings of our media and Congress to crony capitalism, climate anxiety, and China's looming preemptive strike, confidence in our leaders is at an all-time low. This book was written to provide a pathway back to responsible leadership.

CONTENTS

ACKNOWLEDGMENTS

In my first book, I said,

> I don't think it is an over statement to say our political
> pendulum is struggling today. I believe this is largely
> due to slow adoption of the technologies of our times
> by our government and other nonprofit sectors. For
> example, if you add together the number of US senators,
> House of Representatives, president, vice president, the
> Supreme Court, plus a few cabinet members, it adds up
> to around six hundred people. Can six hundred people
> really provide leadership for 350–650 million people in
> a third or fourth Industrial Revolution society without
> advanced feedback and two-way information systems?

In my second book, I also said, "On September 2, 1945 ... all of the
three pendulums of our society peaked with nowhere to go but down."
That was almost eighty years ago. Since then, our voters thrust our noble
six hundred into a new charge every two and four years. Much like the
Light Brigade in 1854, our noble six hundred have faced increasingly
difficult charges as the rest of the world catches up, and the battles wear
on. I would like to acknowledge and thank the noble six hundred who
have made past charges, those charging in office today, and those who
have yet to make the charge.

INTRODUCTION

In President John F. Kennedy's inaugural address on January 20, 1961, he made the following now-famous statements:

> In the long history of the world, only a few generations have been granted the role of defending freedom in its hour of maximum danger. I do not shrink from this responsibility—I welcome it. I do not believe that any of us would exchange places with any other people or any other generation. The energy, the faith, the devotion which we bring to this endeavor will light our country and all who serve it—and the glow from that fire can truly light the world.

> And so, my fellow Americans: ask not what your country can do for you—ask what you can do for your country.

> My fellow citizens of the world: ask not what America will do for you, but what together we can do for the freedom of man.[1]

Over the years, I have come to appreciate President Kennedy's words and understand that he was warning us all against expecting our country to provide for us. We must provide for ourselves and for our country.

Thomas Jefferson gave us many words of guidance in his written letters. These are my favorite:

> Whenever the people are well informed, they can be trusted with their own government; that whenever things get so far wrong as to attract their notice, they may be relied on to set them to rights.[2]

If President Jefferson were alive today, I think he would say things have gotten so wrong that the people must set them to rights. If President Kennedy were alive today, I think he would say we have not heeded his advice. I believe our noble six hundred need the people's help. This book sets forth our pathway to helping our current and future noble six hundred access the great American people through a platform that all can use to come together in a nonthreatening, open forum to debate, analyze, and solve the challenges that confront our nation. Somewhere along the way, we will return the nation to a government by the citizens, rebuild the middle class, and put an end to the lunacy of bifurcating our country between an elite aristocracy and a permanent underclass. Simultaneously, we will defeat climate change and the new Axis powers.

This book builds on my first five books, the courses offered online by the James Michael Matthew Institute, and the James Michael Matthew podcast. I invite you to read my previous books, attend our online courses, and listen to my podcast to prepare for personally participating in future town halls and other events from the Leadership Broadcasting Company.

Why LBC and Why Now?

Our future noble six hundred are doomed to failure before they even take office because they are charging into a sea of unforced errors, and there is a rise in predatory media and predatory helpers.

Charging into a Sea of Unforced Errors

In 1854, the Light Brigade was at least able to begin their charge on dry land and on the battlefield. Our future noble six hundred must begin their charge by jumping into and navigating the sea of unforced errors (see my second book). This sea is already partly filled from eighty years of charges from previous noble six hundred—each one of whom contributed their part to the fill. The following are just a few of the mines that our future noble six hundred will need to navigate in the sea of unforced errors:

- seventy years of half wars (e.g., Korea, Vietnam, Iraq, Afghanistan, Syria, Bay of Pigs, Ukraine, etc.);
- eighty years of deficit spending, accumulated debt, and interest on that debt;
- energy shocks like OPEC and green energy with no transition plan (see my second through fifth books);
- a decline in education competitiveness;
- a messy budget process that is basically nonexistent, hobbling the nation with massive debts (see my second book);
- self-serving power and crossed Rubicon circles that run rampant;
- family feuds and personal conflicts that would have made Alexander Hamilton, Aaron Burr, Al Capone, and Bugsy Malone blush;
- a climate change that is ready to be paid for;
- foreign enemies and challengers;
- a hollowed-out industrial base;
- fifty million dormant workers;
- an aging population; and
- low fertility rates.

Our people are not safe (see my first and second books). They do not trust their institutions. They do not even trust our courts or judicial system. This is a fact that Supreme Court Justices understand, as the court is constantly under blistering attack by partisan forces. In a speech at Kentucky's McConnell Center, Justice Barrett said, "My goal today is to convince you that this court is not comprised of a bunch of partisan hacks."[3] For more examples, read "The 'Stench' of Abortion Politics" from *The American Spectator* and "Yes, Justice Sotomayor, the Court Will 'Survive'" from the *Wall Street Journal*.[4]

The Rise of Predatory Media

The media industry of today is no longer Thomas Jefferson's media (see my second book). Our Constitution was written and our country was founded on the principle that a free and curious press would act as the country's watchdog, keeping our leaders free from mistakes, wrong decisions, and bad ideas. Much of today's media are instead self-serving power predators that constantly circle, entice, coerce, and attack our noble six hundred with withering resources.

Predatory Helpers

As if a sea of unforced errors and a predatory media do not make our valiant six hundred's charge hard enough, they must also battle predatory helpers. These include DC law firms, foreign and domestic lobbyists, consultants, defense contractors, the top of the wealth inequality pyramid, and others commonly referred to as "the swamp." These predatory helpers all have massive resources to battle our noble six hundred's charge.

Why LBC?

My goal is to provide our future noble six hundred and the people of this nation with an open forum and technology platform that can be used as a tool to plan for, debate, and help solve the nation's major problems in an unbiased and nonthreatening environment. Thomas Jefferson was right. The people can be counted on to set things right. All they need is to be informed (knowledge); to have an open debate platform free of hate, fear, self-serving power motivations, and incrimination (trust); and to be listened to after they have spoken (solutions).

Program Cast

The cast for each program will include the following:

- a program host;
- US federal, state, and local legislators;
- US executive branch personnel;
- neighborhood focus groups;
- town hall participants;
- JM Prophecies' teaming partners;
- guest hosts and panels;
- studio audience participants; and
- a national online audience who will vote for questions, advice, and recommendations to be made during the program.

Others can be added as needed, depending on the program and topics.

Case Studies

I have included all the case studies from my previous books in the exhibits. I had planned to combine these in a separate workbook, so you could keep a history of your responses. After monitoring how many chose the e-book option, I decided to include them all here, so you can follow along when the TV programs begin.

1

Channel 1—Building the Climate Change Bridge

THIS CHANNEL WILL consist entirely of filmed documentaries and town hall meetings. Some of these documentaries and meetings will be televised live, and some will be recorded and replayed later. All will be filmed at onsite locations. Channel 1 will provide a platform for viewers to debate, provide feedback, and make decisions during the weekend programming, after each documentary is released. We are still planning the playlist, which will likely continue to change over time, depending on real-time activities and results. However, a sample list of programs for Monday through Sunday is provided. All times are in eastern time.

> ➢ From 6:00 a.m. to 7:00 a.m.—information on building climate change islands and extending the Florida Everglades into the Caribbean, Florida Keys, and Guantanamo Bay

- From 7:00 a.m. to 8:00 a.m.—information on slowing and stopping rising ocean coastlines on the US Atlantic Coast and the Gulf of Mexico

- From 8:00 a.m. to 9:00 a.m.—information on rebuilding freshwater supplies in the Midwest, Mississippi River Valley, and Missouri River Valley

- From 9:00 a.m. to 10:00 a.m.—a morning show about building climate change lakes in the United States

- From 10:00 a.m. to 11:00 a.m.—information on building climate change lakes in Mexico[1]

- From 11:00 a.m. to 12:00 p.m.—information about saving the Great Salt Lake

- From 12:00 p.m. to 1:00 p.m.—information on rebuilding freshwater supplies in the Colorado River Basin and the broader southwest

- From 1:00 p.m. to 2:00 p.m.—information on rebuilding US mountain snowcaps, glaciers, and ice in the Great Lakes.

- From 2:00 p.m. to 3:00 p.m.—an afternoon show about building climate change lakes in the United States

- From 3:00 p.m. to 4:00 p.m.—information on building desalination plants, energy plants, and other infrastructures surrounding North American climate change lakes

- From 4:00 p.m. to 5:00 p.m.—information on the economic development around North American climate change lakes and their shorelines

---

[1] Starting at 9:00 a.m. in Mexico City

➢ From 5:00 p.m. to 6:00 p.m.—information on the economic development around desalinated freshwater supplies from North American climate change lakes

➢ From 6:00 p.m. to 7:00 p.m.—a show hosting federal, state, and local authorities for forums, meetings, and planning discussions

➢ From 7:00 p.m. to 8:00 p.m.—the first hour of LBC town hall meetings

➢ From 8:00 p.m. to 9:00 p.m.—the second hour of LBC town hall meetings

➢ From 9:00 p.m. to 10:00 p.m.—the third hour of LBC town hall meetings

➢ From 10:00 p.m. to 11:00 p.m.—a night show about building climate change lakes in the United States

➢ From 11:00 p.m. to 12:00 a.m.—information on building climate change lakes and climate change islands in South America[2]

➢ From 12:00 a.m. to 1:00 a.m.—information on building climate change islands in Hawaii, Alaska, Midway Island, Wake Island, and Guam[3]

➢ From 1:00 a.m. to 2:00 a.m.—LBC town hall meetings in Africa[4]

---

[2] Starting at 1:00 a.m. in Rio de Janeiro
[3] Starting at 7:00 p.m. in Honolulu
[4] Starting at 7:00 a.m. in Abuja, Nigeria

➤ From 2:00 a.m. to 3:00 a.m.—information on building climate change lakes in deserts in the Middle East[5]

➤ From 3:00 a.m. to 4:00 a.m.—information on building climate change lakes in the Sahara Desert and the Mediterranean Sea[6]

➤ From 4:00 a.m. to 5:00 a.m.—information on building climate change lakes and climate change islands in Australia[7]

➤ From 5:00 a.m. to 6:00 a.m.—LBC town hall meetings in Europe[8]

Partial List of Topics for LBC Town Hall Meetings

A partial list of topics for the LBC town hall meetings for channel 1 are as follows:

- understanding climate change, global warming, net-zero carbon, and how to build the climate change bridge;
- climate change concerns and topics for the local region;
- education of climate change curriculums for middle schools, high schools, and colleges;
- planning for the 2050 land rush;
- emptying prisons and jails onto climate change islands and into climate change lake regions;
- homeless migration onto climate change islands and into climate change lake regions;
- building twenty-first-century monasteries that will transfer, remediate, and cure mental illness through migration to climate change islands and climate change lake regions;

---

[5] Starting at 10:00 a.m. in Bagdad and Riyadh and 9:00 a.m. in Jerusalem

[6] Starting at 9:00 a.m. in Morocco, Rome, and Marseille and 10:00 a.m. in Cairo

[7] Starting at 8:00 p.m. in Sydney

[8] Starting at 10:00 a.m. in London and 11:00 a.m. in Warsaw, Berlin, and Paris

- dividing North American deserts into thirds, leaving untouched desert, salt water climate change lakes, and productive lands with desalinated fresh water;
- energy policy;
- ocean pollution;
- desertification;
- economic impacts of energy policy;
- biodiversity loss;
- megadroughts;
- paying for climate change;
- thermal expansion of the oceans;
- inflation from the war on fossil fuels;
- intergenerational obligations and fairness;
- net-zero carbon;
- the three pendulums of energy policy and ideology;
- geopolitics of climate change, which include defeating the new Axis powers, the strategic atrophy in the United States, and war games that pit *Building the Climate Change Bridge* against past wars (e.g., Afghanistan, Iraq, Syria);
- a ten-time increase in freshwater supplies;
- desalination;
- a discussion of case studies from *Building the Climate Change Bridge, Defeating the New Axis Powers,* and *The Two $20 Trillion Opportunities;*
- how to pay *all* US financial debts and funding entitlements with climate change lakes; and
- keeping flood waters on the lands.

Each town hall meeting will always be led with our primary strategies on how to build the climate change bridge. To be very clear, our primary strategies are to transfer ocean salt waters to the deserts of the world in sufficient quantities to build a centuries-long runway to control rising ocean coastlines; desalinate those transferred salt waters to be used to reverse groundwater and surface freshwater depletion, ultimately increasing the world's usable freshwater supply to 5 percent of the earth's total water; and use that developed infrastructure to reverse biodiversity loss, desertification, and ocean pollution.

2

Channel 2—Defeating the New Axis Powers

PROPHECY ELEVEN: CHINA will launch a preemptive military strike against the United States and its allies.

In my first and second books, I published the "James Michael Matthew Prophecies for the Twenty-First Century." In this book, I am adding prophecy eleven. My prophecy mind tells me that Xi will launch a preemptive military strike during his reign. Exactly when this strike will come is hard to say. Xi's health and life span will play a major part in his decision. For those who believe history repeats itself, my best guess would be sometime between the one-hundredth-year anniversary of Hindenburg's son appointing Adolf Hitler as chancellor and the one-hundredth-year anniversary of the end of World War II. That would be between January 30, 2033, and September 2, 2045. Xi's age during that timeframe would be from seventy-nine to ninety-one.

Channel 2 will consist primarily of filmed documentaries and town hall meetings. Some of these documentaries and town hall meetings will be televised live, and some will be recorded and replayed later. All will be filmed at onsite locations. Channel 2 will provide a platform for viewers to debate, provide feedback and make decisions during the weekend programming, after each documentary is released. We are still planning the playlist, which will likely continue to change over time, depending on real time activities and results. However, a sample list of programs for Monday through Sunday is provided. All times are in eastern time.

➢ From 6:00 a.m. to 7:00 a.m.—a program about how World War III has already begun

➢ From 7:00 a.m. to 8:00 a.m.—defining the sides and alignments of World War III

➢ From 8:00 a.m. to 9:00 a.m.—information on ending strategic atrophy and proving Lenin wrong

➢ From 9:00 a.m. to 10:00 a.m.—information on weapons and technologies of World War III

➢ From 10:00 a.m. to 11:00 a.m.—recruiting and training military and civilian personnel for World War III

➢ From 11:00 a.m. to 12:00 p.m.—information on making the South China Sea economically irrelevant

➢ From 12:00 p.m. to 1:00 p.m.—freedom as a weapon

➢ From 1:00 p.m. to 2:00 p.m.—a one-hundred-thousand-boat-drone navy: the shipbuilding capacity and capability in the United States

➢ From 2:00 p.m. to 3:00 p.m.—the goal of 5 percent fresh water as a weapon

➢ From 3:00 p.m. to 4:00 p.m.—information on China's preemptive strike: the Taiwan campaign

➢ From 4:00 p.m. to 5:00 p.m.—information on China's preemptive strike: the North Pacific campaign

➢ From 5:00 p.m. to 6:00 p.m.—information on US peacetime nuclear power industry

➢ From 6:00 p.m. to 7:00 p.m.—a show hosting federal, state and local authorities for forums, meetings, and planning discussions

➢ From 7:00 p.m. to 8:00 p.m.—the first hour of LBC town hall meetings

➢ From 8:00 p.m. to 9:00 p.m.—the second hour of LBC town hall meetings

➢ From 9:00 p.m. to 10:00 p.m.—information on China's preemptive strike of the US homeland, nuclear weapons, and space war campaigns

➢ From 10:00 p.m. to 11:00 p.m.—raising global awareness of World War III through videogames

➢ From 11:00 p.m. to 12:00 a.m.—information on China's preemptive strike of Mexico, Central America, and South American[9]

➢ From 12:00 a.m. to 1:00 a.m.—information on China's preemptive strike: the Hawaiian Islands campaign[10]

➢ From 1:00 a.m. to 2:00 a.m.—LBC town hall meetings in Africa[11]

---

[9] Starting at 1:00 a.m. in Rio de Janeiro
[10] Starting at 7:00 p.m. in Honolulu
[11] Starting at 7:00 a.m. in Abuja, Nigeria

> From 2:00 a.m. to 3:00 a.m.—information on China's preemptive strike: Middle East desert campaigns[12]

> From 3:00 a.m. to 4:00 a.m.—information on how to destroy China's illegal fishing, drugs, human trafficking, and other illegal economies

> From 4:00 a.m. to 5:00 a.m.—information on China's preemptive strike: the Australia and South Pacific campaigns[13]

> From 5:00 a.m. to 6:00 a.m.—LBC town hall meetings in Europe[14]

---

[12] Starting at 9:00 a.m. in Jerusalem and 10:00 a.m. in Bagdad and Riyadh
[13] Starting at 8:00 p.m. in Sydney
[14] Starting at 10:00 a.m. in London and 11:00 a.m. in Warsaw, Berlin, and Paris

3

Channel 3—Building the Selfless Economy

CHANNEL 3 WILL consist entirely of filmed documentaries and town hall meetings. Some of these documentaries and town hall meetings will be televised live, and some will be recorded and replayed later. All will be filmed at onsite locations. Channel 3 will provide a platform for viewers to debate, provide feedback, and make decisions during the weekend programming, after each documentary is released. We are still planning the playlist, which will likely continue to change over time, depending on real time activities and results. However, a sample list of programs for Monday through Sunday is provided. All times are in eastern time.

➤ From 6:00 a.m. to 7:00 a.m.—big ideas and quests

➤ From 7:00 a.m. to 8:00 a.m.—the first hour of LBC town hall meetings

➤ From 8:00 a.m. to 9:00 a.m.—reindustrialization

➢ From 9:00 a.m. to 10:00 a.m.—information on reviving the dormant workforce

➢ From 10:00 a.m. to 11:00 a.m.—keeping aging populations vibrant and productive

➢ From 11:00 a.m. to 12:00 p.m.—information on how to fix our financial mess

➢ From 12:00 p.m. to 1:00 p.m.—stopping unforced errors

➢ From 1:00 p.m. to 2:00 p.m.—information on health care in America

➢ From 2:00 p.m. to 3:00 p.m.—education business models

➢ From 3:00 p.m. to 4:00 p.m.—ideas, projects, and partnerships

➢ From 4:00 p.m. to 5:00 p.m.—information on moms, dads, families, and family businesses

➢ From 5:00 p.m. to 6:00 p.m.—information on a higher power, the hall of souls, and secular false prophecies

➢ From 6:00 p.m. to 7:00 p.m.—code red

➢ From 7:00 p.m. to 8:00 p.m.—the second hour of LBC town hall meetings

➢ From 8:00 p.m. to 9:00 p.m.—the third hour of LBC town hall meetings

➢ From 9:00 p.m. to 10:00 p.m.—information on criminal justice reform

➢ From 10:00 p.m. to 11:00 p.m.—information on prison reform

➢ From 11:00 p.m. to 12:00 a.m.—feedback for our noble six hundred

➢ From 12:00 a.m. to 1:00 a.m.—information on how to reject self-serving power

➢ From 1:00 a.m. to 2:00 a.m.—LBC town hall meetings in Africa[15]

➢ From 2:00 a.m. to 3:00 a.m.—LBC town hall meetings in the Middle East deserts[16]

➢ From 3:00 a.m. to 4:00 a.m.—LBC town hall meetings in the Sahara Desert and the Mediterranean Sea[17]

➢ From 4:00 a.m. to 5:00 a.m.—LBC town hall meetings in Australia[18]

➢ From 5:00 a.m. to 6:00 a.m.—LBC town hall meetings in Europe[19]

---

[15] Starting at 7:00 a.m. in Abuja, Nigeria
[16] Starting at 9:00 a.m. in Jerusalem and 10:00 a.m. in Bagdad and Riyadh
[17] Starting at 9:00 a.m. in Morocco, Rome, and Marseille and 10:00 a.m. in Cairo
[18] Starting at 8:00 p.m. in Sydney
[19] Starting at 10:00 a.m. in London and 11:00 a.m. in Warsaw, Berlin, and Paris

4

Channel 4—Integrating Western Hemisphere Economies

CHANNEL 4 WILL consist of filmed documentaries; town hall meetings; ideas for business creations, incubators, and economic development; entertainment; regional and local news; information on immigration; and crime and safety statistics.

In chapter 14 of my second book, *Reject Self-Serving Power*, we studied the reasons why immigrants come to the United States. We concluded that the reasons are as follows: economic opportunity, political stability, safety, and respect. Channel 4 will use these reasons as the foundation for program selection and planning. A sample list of programs for Monday through Sunday is provided. All times are in eastern time.

> ➤ From 6:00 a.m. to 7:00 a.m.—information on building a free Cuba through the economic development of Guantanamo Bay

➢ From 7:00 a.m. to 8:00 a.m.—information on how to slow and stop rising ocean coastlines in the Caribbean, South America, and Central America

➢ From 8:00 a.m. to 9:00 a.m.—information on how to build economic partnerships and the integration of Florida and Caribbean nations and territories

➢ From 9:00 a.m. to 10:00 a.m.—information on how to build climate change lakes in South American deserts

➢ From 10:00 a.m. to 11:00 a.m.—raising capital in the western hemisphere to set the foundation for a western hemisphere stock exchange

➢ From 11:00 a.m. to 12:00 p.m.—information on immigration

➢ From 12:00 p.m. to 1:00 p.m.—information on crime and safety

➢ From 1:00 p.m. to 2:00 p.m.—information on how to rebuild mountain snowcaps, freshwater ice, and glaciers in South America

➢ From 2:00 p.m. to 3:00 p.m.—information on how to build maritime and shipbuilding industries in the western hemisphere

➢ From 3:00 p.m. to 4:00 p.m.—partnering with NATO and the European Union

➢ From 4:00 p.m. to 5:00 p.m.—information on economic development around the shorelines of climate change lakes in South America

➢ From 5:00 p.m. to 6:00 p.m.—local country news

➢ From 6:00 p.m. to 7:00 p.m.—a show hosting federal, state, and local authorities from the Caribbean, Mexico, South America, and Central America in forums, meetings and planning discussions

➢ From 7:00 p.m. to 8:00 p.m.—the first hour of LBC town hall meetings

➢ From 8:00 p.m. to 9:00 p.m.—the second hour of LBC town hall meetings

➢ From 9:00 p.m. to 10:00 p.m.—the third hour of LBC town hall meetings

➢ From 10:00 p.m. to 11:00 p.m.—Latin American music and entertainment

➢ From 11:00 p.m. to 12:00 a.m.—TBD or a repeat of the previous recorded programs

➢ From 12:00 a.m. to 1:00 a.m.—TBD or a repeat of the previous recorded programs

➢ From 1:00 a.m. to 2:00 a.m.—TBD or a repeat of the previous recorded programs

➢ From 2:00 a.m. to 3:00 a.m.—TBD or a repeat of the previous recorded programs

➢ From 3:00 a.m. to 4:00 a.m.—TBD or a repeat of the previous recorded programs

➢ From 4:00 a.m. to 5:00 a.m.—TBD or a repeat of the previous recorded programs

> From 5:00 a.m. to 6:00 a.m.—TBD or a repeat of the previous recorded programs

Partial List of Topics for LBC Town Hall Meetings

A partial list of topics for LBC town hall meetings are as follows:

- economic opportunity;
- political stability;
- safety;
- respect;
- monetary policy;
- trade;
- understanding my book *The New Axis Powers;*
- onshoring from China;
- my future book *The Age of Unprecedented Entrepreneurialism;*
- my future book *Building the Selfless Economy;*
- my book *Prophecy before Vision;*
- my book *Reject Self-Serving Power; and*
- my future book *Ideas, Projects, and Businesses.*

Preview

Building the Selfless Economy

THE ELITES NO LONGER HAVE
THE RIGHT STUFF

PERHAPS THEY NEVER DID

Preview

Preemptive Strike

EVENTS TO HAPPEN THINGS TO COME IN WORLD WAR III

Preview

Integrating Western Hemisphere Economies

Integrating Western Hemisphere Economies begins to build the serendipity pools and strategies for how we can finally integrate the economies of the western hemisphere in order to advance all countries in the hemisphere and beyond.

Preview

Crossing Waldo Road

BIRTHPLACE OF THE SELFLESS ECONOMY

Crossing Waldo Road lays out the birthplace of the selfless economy.

Preview

The Western Hemisphere Stock Exchange

LAUNCHING A NEW KIND OF STOCK EXCHANGE

The Western Hemisphere Stock Exchange will provide a new financing pathway for *Integrating Western Hemisphere Economies* and *Building the Selfless Economy.*

Preview

The Next Great Generation

YOUR DESTINY, YOUR PROPHECY, YOUR TIME

Preview

Rebuilding Rural America

Preview

The Age of Unprecedented Entrepreneurialism

Exhibits

Case Studies for My First through Fifth Books

Prophecy before Vision Case Studies: Learning Prophecy

Case Study 1: Criminal Churn

Topic Introduction

The US criminal churn rate approximates seventeen times annually. This level of repeating offenders is overwhelming our judicial system. As a result, judges, prosecutors, and politicians turn to ever-lenient prosecutorial strategies to lessen their caseloads. How can the churn rate best be reduced?

Reader's Topic Analysis

Reader's Conclusions and Recommendations

Case Study 2: Defunding the Police

Topic Introduction

Defunding the police is a topic of great debate. Using the data points presented in prior chapters, please argue both sides: yes, defund the police or no, defunding the police is a detrimental concept and will only make matters worse.

Reader's Topic Analysis

Reader's Conclusions and Recommendations

Case Study 3: Mental Illness

Topic Introduction

During the past several years, the trend has been to close traditional mental health care hospitals and institutions. This trend has arguably led to a massive number of cases where mental illness is not diagnosed or treated. Please provide your analysis of where the country lies as related to mental health care, and also provide any recommendations you may have.

Reader's Topic Analysis

Reader's Conclusions and Recommendations

Case Study 4: Drug Addiction

Topic Introduction

Imagine you are the parent of a twenty-year-old son. He started using drugs at the age of fifteen. Prior to that time, he was a great student, had many friends, and was admired by his younger brother and sister. He has now been a drug addict for five years. He dropped out of high school and stole from you many times to feed his addiction. He has been in and out of rehabilitation four times, each time coming out "clean" but slipping back into addiction. You still love your son, but you and his siblings can no longer believe he will ever get clean. In truth, knowing you all expect him to fail is part of his repeated failures.

Now imagine you are in front of the judge, hearing your son's case for stealing to feed his drug habit. The judge has just informed you of the facilities at JM Prophecies Brain Care. The judge asks your opinions regarding what sentence he should levy on your again-convicted son. What would you recommend?

Case Study 5: Homelessness

Topic Introduction

You are a long-time owner of a beach-front house that you love. You paid $2 million for your house ten years ago. You had it appraised for refinancing two years ago and owe $4 million on a house that appraised for $6 million. An encampment of approximately three hundred homeless people now surrounds your house, practically forcing you into staying inside. You no longer have access to the beach without walking through the encampment. A judge recently ruled that the local police can move the encampment but only if they can be moved to suitable housing.

Imagine your city council is meeting that very night, and you have been asked to testify by your neighborhood watch group. What would you say?

Reader's Topic Analysis

Reader's Conclusions and Recommendations

Case Study 6: Neighborhood Gangs Recruiting Your Children

Topic Introduction

Your son and daughter are both good high school students and never get into trouble. Over the last year, two competing criminal gangs have been recruiting both children to join their gangs or face dire consequences. Both gangs are also recruiting your younger elementary-school-aged children, further threatening your older children in their overall recruitment of all your children. The leaders of both gangs and most members were recently arrested and convicted of multiple crimes. The sentence hearing will be held next week, and the prosecutors have asked you to testify. What would you say?

Reader's Topic Analysis

Reader's Conclusions and Recommendations

Case Study 7: Prisoners' Futures

Topic Introduction

You have been in prison for ten years. You are up for parole. If paroled, you can leave the prison under the oversight of a probation officer. You will have no job and nowhere to go. The parole board offers you the choice of staying in prison in one of JM Prophecies Brain Care's concentric villages of squares or going free onto the street. What would you ask for the board to clarify about JM Prophecies Brain Care, and what would you do?

Reader's Topic Analysis

Reader's Conclusions and Recommendations

Case Study 8: Prisoner's Family Members

Topic Introduction

You are the wife of a man currently in prison. He has been in prison for five years and has five more years to serve. His prison has entered into an agreement with JM Prophecies Brain Care. You and your children will have the opportunity to move into one of the JM Prophecies Brain Care's villages. What would you ask about JM Prophecies Brain Care, and what would you do?

Reader's Topic Analysis

Reader's Conclusions and Recommendations

Case Study 9: Entrepreneurs Relocating into a JM Prophecies Brain Care Village

Topic Introduction

You are an entrepreneur. You have identified a company that you would like to purchase and become the CEO of, but you need external financing to complete the transaction. An affiliate of JM Prophecies has agreed to finance your acquisition with the requirement that you locate the company in a JM Prophecies concentric village, which would place you and your employees next to a prison. What would you do?

Reader's Topic Analysis

Reader's Conclusions and Recommendations

Case Study 10: CEO Prophecy

Topic Introduction

You have read *Prophecy before Vision* and understand its power. What are your type I prophecies? What are your type II prophecies? How do you plan to publish your prophecies with your investors and board of directors? How will you articulate your updated vision to your employees?

Reader's Topic Analysis

Reader's Conclusions and Recommendations

Case Study 11: ESG Fund Manager

Topic Introduction

You have read *Prophecy before Vision* and understand its power. How will your prophecies alter your investment strategies, if at all?

Reader's Topic Analysis

Reader's Conclusions and Recommendations

Case Study 12: CEO—the Technologies of the Times

Topic Introduction

What do you consider to be the technologies of the times? How do you plan for them in your organization?

Reader's Topic Analysis

Reader's Conclusions and Recommendations

Case Study 13: CEO Prophecy—Three Pendulum Fissures

Topic Introduction

Do you believe there are any material fissures in the three pendulums of a society that will impact your organization? If yes, what are they?

Reader's Topic Analysis

Reader's Conclusions and Recommendations

Case Study 14: CEO Prophecy—Serendipity Pools

Topic Introduction

You are the CEO of an international trading company. What serendipity pools and strategy are you planning to recommend to your senior management team?

Reader's Topic Analysis

Reader's Conclusions and Recommendations

Case Study 15: Marketing Senior Vice President—Prophecy

Topic Introduction

You have read *Prophecy before Vision* and understand its power. Your CEO has published his prophecies and has asked how to look at them from a marketing perspective. How will you articulate your thoughts to your CEO?

Reader's Topic Analysis

Reader's Conclusions and Recommendations

Case Study 16: CEO and Board of Directors—Prophecy for China

Topic Introduction

At your collective strategy, decision, and direction, your company has made a big bet, investing in China. You obviously disagree with JM Prophecies' strategy and James Michael Matthew's first and fourth prophecies. Why do you disagree? What will happen to your company if you bet wrong?

Reader's Topic Analysis

Reader's Conclusions and Recommendations

Case Study 17: CEO and Board of Directors— Prophecy for Green Energy Economy

Topic Introduction

How do you see the conversion of an economy based on fossil fuel energy to one based on green energy playing out in the United States and globally? What serendipity pools have you positioned for the coming of a green energy economy? What bets are you considering for pendulum swings created by the conversion? How are you positioning your company on the inside of the pendulum?

Case Study 18: CEO and Board of Directors—Prophecy—Aging Populations

Topic Introduction

Have you published any prophecies regarding the aging of populations? If you did, what are they, and why did you pick them? If not, why not?

Reader's Topic Analysis

Reader's Conclusions and Recommendations

Case Study 19: CEO and Board of Directors—Prophecy—Studying and Analyzing Global Demographics

Topic Introduction

Does your company have an established methodology and forecasting policy for monitoring, analyzing, and forecasting global demographics? If you don't, why not? If you do, what are they? Do you maintain an actuarial chain-link historical forecasting model? If not, why not? If you did, how accurate has it been in predicting the future?

Reader's Topic Analysis

Case Study 20: CEO and Board of Directors—Prophecy—Things to Come

Topic Introduction

Have you published a list of "things to come" actions that you plan to take to alter the future? If you have, what are they? If not, why not? Do you believe you should reconsider?

Reader's Topic Analysis

Reader's Conclusions and Recommendations

Case Study 21: CEO and Board of Directors—Prophecy—Serendipity Pools

Topic Introduction

Have you ever discussed the concept of serendipity pools in any board meetings? If not, would you or should you? Why or why not?

Reader's Topic Analysis

Reader's Conclusions and Recommendations

Case Study 22: CEO and Board of Directors— Prophecy—a Higher Power

Topic Introduction

Have you ever discussed the concept of a higher power in any board meetings? If not, would you or should you? Why or why not?

Reader's Topic Analysis

Reader's Conclusions and Recommendations

Case Study 23: CEO and Board of Directors— Prophecy—Technologies of the Times

Topic Introduction

Have you published a list of the technologies of the times? If not, why not? If you have, what does the list look like?

Reader's Topic Analysis

Reader's Conclusions and Recommendations

Case Study 24: CEO and Board of Directors— Prophecy—Swings in the Civil Society Pendulum

Topic Introduction

Do you analyze and make predictions for the swings in the civil society pendulum? If not, why not? If you do, what would such a list of predictions look like?

Reader's Topic Analysis

Reader's Conclusions and Recommendations

Case Study 25: CEO and Board of Directors—*Prophecy before Vision*

Topic Introduction

After reading and studying *Prophecy before Vision*, do you believe it is possible for you to see and predict the future? Do you believe that there are "events to happen" as described in the book, that these events will happen, and that nothing can be done to change or prevent them? Do you believe that you can alter the future through the concept of "things to come"? Do you believe you and your people can always be the smartest people in the room? Do you believe you can make the right decision every time, with only 10 percent of the information? Do you believe there are signs from a higher power to guide you if you act for the good? For each of these questions, please explain why or why not. If you said yes, would you always have said yes?

Reader's Topic Analysis

Reader's Conclusions and Recommendations

Reject Self-Serving Power Case Studies:
Helping Others Be Successful

Case Study 1: Doing Business in China

Topic Introduction

You are the chair of a publicly traded company that is listed and actively traded on a US stock exchange. You recently read a book that documented the scrutiny and legal and criminal liability incurred by large Japanese companies after World War II. You also read the one-hundredth-anniversary threat made to the world by the Chinese Communist Party. Your company recently made a large investment in China. What are you thinking, and what should you do? Would your answer change if China invaded Taiwan and/or launched a nuclear attack on Japan?

Reader's Topic Analysis

Reader's Conclusions and Recommendations

Case Study 2: Doing Business in China

Topic Introduction

Your CPA firm is the independent auditor of the company described in case study 1. You are the engagement partner. You have also read the same materials that the chair has read. What should you do? Has the company included any risk factors for these potential issues in their SEC filings about their operations in China? If they have, what are they? If not, why not? Would your answer change if China invaded Taiwan and/or launched a nuclear attack on Japan?

Reader's Topic Analysis

Reader's Conclusions and Recommendations

Case Study 3: Doing Business in China

Topic Introduction

Your law firm is the lead SEC counsel for the company described in case study 1. You are the engagement partner. You have also read the same materials that the chair has read. What should you do? Has the company included any risk factors for these potential issues in their SEC filings about their operations in China? If so, what are they? If not, why not? Would your answer change if China invaded Taiwan and/or launched a nuclear attack on Japan?

Reader's Topic Analysis

Reader's Conclusions and Recommendations

Case Study 4: Target Markets at the Bottom of the Wealth Inequality Pyramid

Topic Introduction

You are the owner of a private company in the United States. You have read both my first and second books. You are willing to assess whether these could be potential target markets for your company. Where do you begin your assessment?

Reader's Topic Analysis

_____

Reader's Conclusions and Recommendations

_____

Case Study 5: JM Prophecies Brain Care Corporation

Topic Introduction

You are the governor of a state. Your state is suffering under a wave of crime. You are up for reelection and plan to run for another term. You have read my first and second books and are wondering if the proposals for both prison reform and clearing your state of crime could be viable solutions for you and your state. What should you do? How do you plan to make your initial assessments?

Reader's Topic Analysis

_____

Reader's Conclusions and Recommendations

_____

Case Study 6: JM Prophecies Brain Care Corporation

Topic Introduction

You are the attorney general of a state. Your state is suffering under a wave of crime. You are up for reelection and plan to run for another term. You have read my first and second books and are wondering if the proposals for both prison reform and clearing your state of crime could be viable solutions for you and your state. What should you do? How do you plan to make your initial assessments?

Reader's Topic Analysis

Reader's Conclusions and Recommendations

Case Study 7: JM Prophecies Brain Care Corporation

Topic Introduction

You are the warden of a large state prison. Your prison has a severe inmate aging issue. You have read both my first and second books. You are wondering if the proposal for prison reform as proposed by JM Prophecies Brain Care Corporation could be a viable solution for your prison. What should you do? How do you plan to make your initial assessments?

Reader's Topic Analysis

Reader's Conclusions and Recommendations

Case Study 8: JM Prophecies' Leadership Code

Topic Introduction

You are the CEO of a publicly traded company. You have read the information and understand my discussions of the JM Prophecies' leadership code. You are deciding if this leadership approach could be a fit for your company. What are your next steps?

Case Study 9: JM Prophecies' Leadership Code

Topic Introduction

You are the managing partner of a large investment firm. You have read the information and understand my discussions of the JM Prophecies' leadership code. You are deciding if this leadership approach could be a fit for your portfolio companies. What are your next steps?

Reader's Topic Analysis

Reader's Conclusions and Recommendations

Case Study 10: JM Prophecies' Leadership Code

Topic Introduction

You are the founder and sole owner of a private manufacturing company. You have read the information and understand my discussions of the JM Prophecies' leadership code. You disagree with my strategies for helping others be successful, instead believing you should make all the important decisions. You have a large bank loan, and the bank has asked if you are familiar with my works. What would you say?

Reader's Topic Analysis

Reader's Conclusions and Recommendations

Case Study 11: JM Prophecies' Leadership Code

Topic Introduction

You are the banker of the company in case study 10. You have read the information and understand my discussions of the JM Prophecies' leadership code. You agree with my strategies for helping others to be successful, but the CEO and owner disagree. What would you say?

Reader's Topic Analysis

Reader's Conclusions and Recommendations

Case Study 12: Self-Serving Power

Topic Introduction

You are a member of a state legislature. Your family has had a long and successful political career. Your family has always operated with a ruthless, self-serving strategy. Your enemies have been plotting your family's demise. You have read *Reject Self-Serving Power* and want to have an open family discussion about your futures. What should you do and say?

Reader's Topic Analysis

Reader's Conclusions and Recommendations

Case Study 13: JM Prophecies' Decision-Making Equation

Topic Introduction

Assume that the same circumstances as case study 12 are true here. What would your JM Prophecies' decision-making equation look like?

Reader's Topic Analysis

Reader's Conclusions and Recommendations

Case Study 14: Rubicon Circles of Power and Time

Topic Introduction

Assume that the same circumstances as case study 12 are true here. How would you assess your Rubicon circles?

Reader's Topic Analysis

Reader's Conclusions and Recommendations

Case Study 15: Sea of Unforced Errors

Topic Introduction

Assume that the same circumstances as case study 12 are true here. What would your list of past mistakes, wrong decisions, and bad ideas for your family potentially look like? What would the list potentially look like for your enemies?

Reader's Topic Analysis

Reader's Conclusions and Recommendations

Case Study 16: Looking at Leadership through the Lens of the Bottom of the Wealth Inequality Pyramid

Topic Introduction

You are the CEO of a large private company. You have read my plea to look at these target market segments. What would you say and do?

Reader's Topic Analysis

Reader's Conclusions and Recommendations

Case Study 17: Looking at Leadership through the Lens of the Bottom of the Wealth Inequality Pyramid

Topic Introduction

You are the governor of a large state. You have read my plea to look at and study what JM Prophecies Brain Care Corporation is all about. You have also read my assertion that it is time to make our neighborhoods and country safe and to reform our outrageous prison system. You are currently assessing my claim that these two goals are *not* mutually exclusive and that we can solve both problems together at the same time. What are your assessments so far? What further questions do you have?

Reader's Topic Analysis

Reader's Conclusions and Recommendations

Case Study 18: Inequality Economics

Topic Introduction
You are on the staff of the Congressional Budget Office (CBO). You have read my proposal for inequality economics. What do you think?

Reader's Topic Analysis

Reader's Conclusions and Recommendations

Case Study 19: Reindustrialization of the United States

Topic Introduction
You are the CEO of a large publicly traded manufacturing company based in the United States. You have received an invitation from me to enter into a team agreement. What will you do?

Case Study 20: Circle of Life Retirement Strategy

Topic Introduction

You serve as an advisor to the board of trustees for social security. You have read my recommendations for legislative changes to convert linear cliff retirement to a circle of life. What will you tell the board? What do you think they will say?

Reader's Topic Analysis

Reader's Conclusions and Recommendations

Case Study 21: Big Ideas, Quests, and Journeys

Topic Introduction

You serve on the board of a large think tank. You have read my chapter on big ideas, quests, and journeys. Do you have any ideas to bring to the pipeline? If so, what are they?

Reader's Topic Analysis

Reader's Conclusions and Recommendations

Case Study 22: Integrating Western Hemisphere Economies

Topic Introduction

You are the president of a midsized Latin American country. You have read my chapter on integrating western hemisphere economies. What are your thoughts?

Reader's Topic Analysis

Reader's Conclusions and Recommendations

Case Study 23: Reversing Time on the US Debt Clock

Topic Introduction

You are on the staff of a state governor, with responsibilities for assessing both your state's and the federal government's budget process. Have you historically used the US debt clock? If so, how do you use it? If not, why not?

Reader's Topic Analysis

Reader's Conclusions and Recommendations

Case Study 24: It's Not about Race; It's about Leadership

Topic Introduction

You are an alderman for the city of Chicago. You have read my first two books and want to ask me to speak to the city council. What are the areas you want me to discuss?

Reader's Topic Analysis

Reader's Conclusions and Recommendations

Case Study 25: Leadership Broadcasting Corporation

Topic Introduction

You are the CEO of a large media company. You have read the preview for my ninth book. What do you think?

Reader's Topic Analysis

Reader's Conclusions and Recommendations

Building the Climate Change Bridge
Case Studies: Learning How to Build the Climate Change Bridge

Case Study 1: Net-Zero Carbon

Topic Introduction
Define and discuss your understanding of net-zero carbon.

Reader's Topic Analysis

_____

Reader's Conclusions and Recommendations

_____

Case Study 2: Climate Change Knowledge

Topic Introduction
Define and discuss your understanding of rising ocean coastlines.

Reader's Topic Analysis

_____

Reader's Conclusions and Recommendations

_____

Case Study 3: Climate Change Knowledge

Topic Introduction
Define and discuss your understanding of biodiversity loss.

Reader's Topic Analysis

Reader's Conclusions and Recommendations

Case Study 4: Climate Change Knowledge

Topic Introduction
Define and discuss your understanding of desertification.

Reader's Topic Analysis

Reader's Conclusions and Recommendations

Case Study 5: Climate Change Knowledge

Topic Introduction
Define and discuss your understanding of ocean thermal expansion.

Reader's Topic Analysis

Reader's Conclusions and Recommendations

Case Study 6: Climate Change Knowledge

Topic Introduction
Define and discuss your understanding of groundwater and surface freshwater depletion.

Reader's Topic Analysis

Reader's Conclusions and Recommendations

Case Study 7: Three Pendulums of Energy Policy and Ideology

Topic Introduction

Explain how the three pendulums of energy policy work and how they are changing the evolution of the green energy industry.

Reader's Topic Analysis

Reader's Conclusions and Recommendations

Case Study 8: New Axis Powers

Topic Introduction

Do you agree with the author's assessment of the new Axis powers and their weaponization of energy? Why or why not?

Reader's Topic Analysis

Reader's Conclusions and Recommendations

Case Study 9: Russia's Invasion of Ukraine

Topic Introduction

Do you believe Russia's invasion of Ukraine has changed the green energy industry and movement? Why or why not?

Reader's Topic Analysis

Reader's Conclusions and Recommendations

Case Study 10: Desalination Industry

Topic Introduction

Define and discuss your understanding of the current state of the desalination industry.

Reader's Topic Analysis

Reader's Conclusions and Recommendations

Case Study 11: Ocean Pollution

Topic Introduction

What do you believe are the most important ocean pollutions to resolve? Why?

Reader's Topic Analysis

Reader's Conclusions and Recommendations

Case Study 12: Energy Economics

Topic Introduction

Please discuss your understanding of how energy policy impacts inflation and global economies.

Reader's Topic Analysis

Reader's Conclusions and Recommendations

Case Study 13: Intergenerational Obligations and Fairness

Topic Introduction

Discuss what you believe are reasonable goals for your generation's obligations and environmental fairness to future generations.

Reader's Topic Analysis

Reader's Conclusions and Recommendations

Case Study 14: US Supreme Court's Decision on EPA Regulations

Topic Introduction
Discuss your understanding of the Supreme Court's decision to restrict the Environmental Protection Agency's power to regulate carbon emissions that cause climate change.

Reader's Topic Analysis

Reader's Conclusions and Recommendations

Case Study 15: US Supreme Court's Decision on EPA

Topic Introduction
What impact do you believe the Supreme Court's decision on EPA regulations will have on the Securities and Exchange Commission's rules for environmental disclosure or other agencies, such as the USDA?

Reader's Topic Analysis

Reader's Conclusions and Recommendations

Case Study 16: Green Energy Advocates' Rubicon Circles of Power and Time

Topic Introduction
Explain your understanding of the author's discussion of green energy Rubicon circles of power and time. Do you agree with his assessment? Why or why not?

Reader's Topic Analysis

_____

Reader's Conclusions and Recommendations

_____

Case Study 17: Globalization

Topic Introduction

Discuss the role of globalization in green energy policy.

Reader's Topic Analysis

_____

Reader's Conclusions and Recommendations

_____

Case Study 18: Globalization

Topic Introduction

Do you agree that globalization is essentially dead? Why or why not?

Reader's Topic Analysis

_____

Reader's Conclusions and Recommendations

_____

Case Study 19: Conclusions, Solutions, and Recommendations

Topic Introduction

Read and discuss chapter 21 of the author's second book, commenting specifically on the author's calculations.

Reader's Topic Analysis

Reader's Conclusions and Recommendations

Case Study 20: Conclusions, Solutions, and Recommendations

Topic Introduction

Do you believe that the author's conclusions, solutions, and recommendations are viable and reasonable enough to establish future climate change policy upon? Why or why not?

Reader's Topic Analysis

Reader's Conclusions and Recommendations

Case Study 21: Conclusions, Solutions, and Recommendations

Topic Introduction

What enhancements or changes would you make to the author's plan?

Reader's Topic Analysis

Reader's Conclusions and Recommendations

Case Study 22: Primary Strategies to Build the Climate Change Bridge

Topic Introduction

Do you believe that there does not currently exist a plan to solve climate change or transition from fossil fuels to alternative energies? Why or why not?

Reader's Topic Analysis

Reader's Conclusions and Recommendations

Case Study 23: Primary Strategies to Build the Climate Change Bridge

Topic Introduction

Discuss the author's three primary strategies to build the climate change bridge, as outlined in chapter 13. Include your agreement or disagreement of their viability.

Reader's Topic Analysis

Reader's Conclusions and Recommendations

Case Study 24: Paying for the Climate Change Bridge

Topic Introduction

Do you agree with the author's plan to pay for the climate change bridge from chapter 21 of his second book? Why or why not?

Reader's Topic Analysis

Reader's Conclusions and Recommendations

Case Study 25: Paying for the Climate Change Bridge

Topic Introduction

Please list your recommendations for paying for the climate change bridge.

Reader's Topic Analysis

Reader's Conclusions and Recommendations

Case Study 26: Competitive Energy Technologies and Energy Diversification

Topic Introduction

Do you agree with the author's discussion of competitive energy technologies and energy diversification? Why or why not?

Reader's Topic Analysis

Reader's Conclusions and Recommendations

Case Study 27: The Great Water Opportunity from Global Warming

Topic Introduction

Do you agree with the author's discussion of the great water opportunity from global warming? Why or why not?

Reader's Topic Analysis

_____

Reader's Conclusions and Recommendations

_____

Defeating the New Axis Powers
Case Studies: World War III War Games

Case Study 1: Geopolitics of Climate Change

Topic Introduction

Do you agree that energy policy must consider both climate change and geopolitics? Why or why not? Do you agree that the new Axis powers are more than happy to play along with the West, under the pretense of caring about achieving net-zero carbon, while all along weaponizing fossil fuels and raw materials for green energy? Why or why not?

Reader's Topic Analysis

_____

Reader's Conclusions and Recommendations

_____

Case Study 2: Geopolitics of Climate Change

Topic Introduction

Do you agree that defeating the new Axis powers must always take precedent over defeating global warming? Why or why not?

Reader's Topic Analysis

_____

Reader's Conclusions and Recommendations

_____

Case Study 3: World War III

Topic Introduction

Do you agree that World War III has already begun? Why or why not?

Reader's Topic Analysis

_____

Reader's Conclusions and Recommendations

_____

Case Study 4: New Axis Powers

Topic Introduction

Do you agree that the new Axis powers have been formed? Do you believe these countries coordinate and plot against the United States and its allies? Do you agree with the author's definition of the opposing sides? Do you believe that the Allies must battle and defeat the new Axis powers? Why or why not?

Reader's Topic Analysis

_____

Reader's Conclusions and Recommendations

_____

Case Study 5: New Axis Powers

Topic Introduction

Do you agree that the new Axis powers have weaponized fossil fuels and energy against the Allies? Why or why not?

Reader's Topic Analysis

Reader's Conclusions and Recommendations

Case Study 6: Conventional Warfare

Topic Introduction

Do you believe that conventional warfare no longer works? Why or why not?

Reader's Topic Analysis

Reader's Conclusions and Recommendations

Case Study 7: Strategic Atrophy

Topic Introduction

Do you believe our country suffers from strategic atrophy? Why or why not? Discuss your understanding of strategic atrophy. What strategies to solve it would you suggest?

Reader's Topic Analysis

Reader's Conclusions and Recommendations

Case Study 8: No Longer Such a Thing as War or Peace

Topic Introduction

Do you believe that there is no such thing as war or peace but that both coexist? Why or why not? Do you agree that the new Axis powers render net-zero carbon a useless strategy? Do you believe that ESG investing based on carbon emissions is useless?

Reader's Topic Analysis

Reader's Conclusions and Recommendations

Case Study 9: World War III Geographic Theaters

Topic Introduction

Do you agree with the author's discussions of World War III geographic theaters? Why or why not?

Reader's Topic Analysis

Reader's Conclusions and Recommendations

Case Study 10: World War III Geographic Theaters

Topic Introduction

Do you agree that the United States needs to continue to expand its global base readiness, not reduce it? Why or why not?

Reader's Topic Analysis

Reader's Conclusions and Recommendations

Case Study 11: World War III Geographic Theaters

Topic Introduction

Do you agree that climate change lakes and islands can serve to expand World War III battlefields in favor of the Allies? Why or why not?

Reader's Topic Analysis

Reader's Conclusions and Recommendations

Case Study 12: Nuclear Power

Topic Introduction

Do you agree that the West needs to get back into nuclear energy in a big way? Why or why not?

Reader's Topic Analysis

Reader's Conclusions and Recommendations

Case Study 13: Nuclear Power

Topic Introduction

Do you agree that nuclear energy facilities ultimately make nuclear weapon designs and advancements? Why or why not?

Reader's Topic Analysis

Reader's Conclusions and Recommendations

Case Study 14: Military Personnel Recruiting

Topic Introduction

Do you agree that the military should lead in recruiting practices to start new military families? Why or why not? Do you agree that the military should have a standing reserve of millions or tens of millions under short-term service and should recruit those millions from the bottom of the wealth inequality pyramid? Why or why not?

Reader's Topic Analysis

Reader's Conclusions and Recommendations

Case Study 15: Economic Strategies and Alignments

Topic Introduction

Do you agree with the author's assessments of economic strategies and alignments in chapter 7? Why or why not?

Reader's Topic Analysis

_____

Reader's Conclusions and Recommendations

_____

Case Study 16: Freedom as a Weapon

Topic Introduction

Do you agree with the author's assessments and recommendations for using freedom as a weapon in chapter 8? Why or why not?

Reader's Topic Analysis

_____

Reader's Conclusions and Recommendations

_____

Case Study 17: Global Demographics

Topic Introduction

Do you agree with the author's discussions and prophecies of China's demographics in chapter 9? Why or why not?

Reader's Topic Analysis

_____

Reader's Conclusions and Recommendations

_____

Case Study 18: Left-Wing Green Energy Ideology

Topic Introduction

Do you agree that the left-wing green energy crowd has hijacked the green energy movement to advance their wealth and self-serving power? Why or why not?

Reader's Topic Analysis

Reader's Conclusions and Recommendations

Case Study 19: Left-Wing Green Energy Ideology

Topic Introduction

Do you agree that the green energy and fossil fuel pendulums are swinging wildly in all directions but that eventually these swings will stabilize? Why or why not?

Reader's Topic Analysis

Reader's Conclusions and Recommendations

Case Study 20: Net-Zero Carbon Goals and Outcomes

Topic Introduction

Do you agree with the author's discussion in chapter 10 about educating the world on global warming and climate change? Explain why or why not, specifically discussing net-zero carbon.

Reader's Topic Analysis

Reader's Conclusions and Recommendations

Case Study 21: Prophecies for World War III

Topic Introduction

Do you agree with the author's prophecies for World War III, as discussed in chapter 13? Why or why not?

Reader's Topic Analysis

Reader's Conclusions and Recommendations

Case Study 22: Prophecies for World War III

Topic Introduction

What additional prophecies would you make for World War III?

Reader's Topic Analysis

Reader's Conclusions and Recommendations

Case Study 23: Serendipity Pools for World War III

Topic Introduction

Do you agree with the author's serendipity pools for World War III, as discussed in chapter 13? Why or why not?

Reader's Topic Analysis

Reader's Conclusions and Recommendations

Case Study 24: Serendipity Pools for World War III

Topic Introduction

What different serendipity pools would you make for World War III?

Reader's Topic Analysis

Reader's Conclusions and Recommendations

Case Study 25: JM Prophecies Corporation Defense Business

Topic Introduction

Please prepare a SWOT analysis of the JM Prophecies Corporation defense business, as discussed in chapter 14.

Reader's Topic Analysis

Reader's Conclusions and Recommendations

The Two $20 Trillion Opportunities
Case Studies: Learning the Two
$20 Trillion Opportunities

Case Study 1: Goal of 5 Percent Usable Fresh Water

Topic Introduction
Explain your understanding of the goal of 5 percent usable fresh water.

Reader's Topic Analysis

Reader's Conclusions and Recommendations

Case Study 2: Goal of 5 Percent Usable Fresh Water

Topic Introduction
Do you agree with the author's recommendation that the freshwater goal should be the top climate change goal? Why or why not?

Reader's Topic Analysis

Reader's Conclusions and Recommendations

Case Study 3: Goal of 5 Percent Usable Fresh Water

Topic Introduction
Do you agree that the hurdle test for the thirty-year mortgage is a fair test to benchmark global warming strategies against? Why or why not?

Reader's Topic Analysis

Reader's Conclusions and Recommendations

Case Study 4: Goal of 5 Percent Usable Fresh Water

Topic Introduction

Do you believe the freshwater goal is a politically viable and consensus-building strategy? Why or why not?

Reader's Topic Analysis

Reader's Conclusions and Recommendations

Case Study 5: Goal of 5 Percent Usable Fresh Water

Topic Introduction

Do you agree that the freshwater goal is the best path forward for helping developing countries' global warming transition? Why or why not?

Reader's Topic Analysis

Reader's Conclusions and Recommendations

Case Study 6: Goal of 5 Percent Usable Fresh Water

Topic Introduction

Explain the author's position on the idea that the freshwater goal is a direct strategy that goes on offense, but net-zero carbon is an indirect strategy that is purely defensive. Do you agree with the author? Why or why not?

Reader's Topic Analysis

_____

Reader's Conclusions and Recommendations

_____

Case Study 7: Climate Change Lakes and Islands

Topic Introduction

Explain the author's strategy for climate change lakes and islands. Do you believe this is a viable strategy? Why or why not?

Reader's Topic Analysis

_____

Reader's Conclusions and Recommendations

_____

Case Study 8: Ocean Water Transfer Credits

Topic Introduction

Explain the concept of ocean water transfer credits and how you believe they are envisioned to work.

Reader's Topic Analysis

Reader's Conclusions and Recommendations

Case Study 9: Ocean Water Transfer Credits

Topic Introduction

Compare and contrast ocean water transfer credits against carbon transfer credits and carbon offsets. Include your opinion of their relative values.

Reader's Topic Analysis

Reader's Conclusions and Recommendations

Case Study 10: Super-Emitters

Topic Introduction

Explain super-emitters.

Reader's Topic Analysis

Reader's Conclusions and Recommendations

Case Study 11: Land Rushes for Climate Change Lakes and Islands

Topic Introduction

Do you agree with the author's strategy and tactics for land rushes? Why or why not?

Reader's Topic Analysis

_____

Reader's Conclusions and Recommendations

_____

Case Study 12: Positives from Global Warming

Topic Introduction

Do you believe there are positives from global warming that should be retained if possible? If so, what are they? If not, why not?

Reader's Topic Analysis

_____

Reader's Conclusions and Recommendations

_____

Case Study 13: Paying for Climate Change

Topic Introduction

Explain the strengths and weaknesses of the author's recommendations for paying for climate change.

Reader's Topic Analysis

Reader's Conclusions and Recommendations

Case Study 14: Paying for Climate Change

Topic Introduction

List and explain your recommendations for how to best pay for climate change.

Reader's Topic Analysis

Reader's Conclusions and Recommendations

Case Study 15: The Selfless Economy

Topic Introduction

Explain your understanding of the selfless economy.

Reader's Topic Analysis

Reader's Conclusions and Recommendations

Case Study 16: Community Leadership Layering

Topic Introduction
Explain your understanding of community leadership layering.

Reader's Topic Analysis

Reader's Conclusions and Recommendations

Case Study 17: Clubhouse Incubators

Topic Introduction
Explain your understanding of clubhouse incubators.

Reader's Topic Analysis

Reader's Conclusions and Recommendations

Case Study 18: Ending Crime and Prison Life

Topic Introduction
Do you agree that both crime and prison life can be stopped by building climate change lakes and islands? Why or why not?

Reader's Topic Analysis

Reader's Conclusions and Recommendations

Case Study 19: Self-Assembling in Nature

Topic Introduction
Explain your understanding of self-assembling technologies.

Reader's Topic Analysis

Reader's Conclusions and Recommendations

Case Study 20: Military Strategic Atrophy

Topic Introduction
Explain your understanding of military strategic atrophy.

Reader's Topic Analysis

Reader's Conclusions and Recommendations

Case Study 21: Paying Our Debts

Topic Introduction
Prepare an analysis of the section "Paying Our Debts and Fixing Our Financial Mess" from chapter 21.

Reader's Topic Analysis

Reader's Conclusions and Recommendations

REFERENCES

1 "Ask Not What Your Country Can Do for You," Washington, D.C., transcript and video recording, 4:17, https://www.ushistory.org/documents/ask-not.htm. Retrieved 9/14/2021.

2 "Thomas Jefferson Papers," Library of Congress, 1606–1827, https://www.loc.gov/collections/thomas-jefferson-papers/articles-and-essays/selected-quotations-from-the-thomas-jefferson-papers/.

3 Daniel Henninger, "Can Stephen Breyer and Amy Coney Barrett Save the Supreme Court?" *Wall Street Journal*, September 15, 2021, https://www.wsj.com/articles/supreme-court-packing-justice-breyer-barrett-biden-squad-tinker-roe-abortion-politicized-11631738719. Retrieved 4/14/2023.

4 George Neumayr, December 1, 2021, https://spectator.org/the-stench-of-abortion-politics/; Crispin Sartwell, December 3, 2021, https://www.wsj.com/articles/justice-sotomayor-supreme-court-abortion-politicization-mississippi-dobbs-jackson-15-weeks-11638554054?mod=mhp.

BIBLIOGRAPHY

Henninger, Daniel. "Can Stephen Breyer and Amy Coney Barrett Save the Supreme Court?" Wall Street Journal, September 15, 2021. https://www.wsj.com/articles/supreme-court-packing-justice-brey er-barrett-biden-squad-tinker-roe-abortion-politicized-11631738719.

Jefferson, Thomas. "Thomas Jefferson Papers." Library of Congress, 1606–1827. https://www.loc.gov/collections/thomas-jefferson-papers/ articles-and-essays/selected-quotations-from-the-thomas-jefferson-papers/.

Kennedy, John F. "Ask Not What Your Country Can Do For You." Inaugural address. Washington, D.C. January 20, 1961. Transcript and video recording, 4 min., 17 sec. https://www.ushistory.org/ documents/ask-not.htm.

Neumayr, George. "The 'Stench' of Abortion Politics." *The American Spectator*, December 1, 2021. https://spectator.org/the-stench-of-abortion-politics/.

Sartwell, Crispin "Yes, Justice Sotomayor, the Court Will 'Survive.'" *Wall Street Journal*, December 3, 2021. https://www.wsj.com/articles/justic e-sotomayor-supreme-court-abortion-politicization-mississippi-dobbs-jackson-15-weeks-11638554054?mod=mhp.